Earth-Friendly Shopping

Gillian Gosman

PowerKiDS
press.
New York

Published in 2011 by The Rosen Publishing Group, Inc.
29 East 21st Street, New York, NY 10010

First Edition

Editor: Joanne Randolph
Book Design: Kate Laczynski

Photo Credits: Cover © www.iStockphoto.com/RonTech2000; pp. 4, 18, 21 Hemera/ Thinkstock; p. 5 Frank Polich/Bloomberg/Getty Images; p. 6 Digital Vision/Thinkstock; pp. 7, 23, 24 Shutterstock.com; p. 8 Thinkstock Images/Comstock/Thinkstock; p. 9 JGI/Jamie Grill/Getty Images; pp. 10–11 Jeff Haynes/AFP/Getty Images; p. 12 Mark Thompson/Getty Images; p. 13 Robert Nickelsberg/Getty Images; p. 14 Wally Eberhart/ Getty Images; p. 15 Tom Brakefield/Getty Images; p. 16 Russell Sadur/Getty Images; p. 17 Jim R. Bounds/Bloomberg/Getty Images; p. 19 Thomas Northcut/Getty Images; p. 20 (top) © www.iStockphoto.com/Kristina Smirnova; p. 20 (bottom) Ciaran Griffin/ Stockbyte/Thinkstock; p. 22 SSPL/Getty Images; p. 25 Jerry Pavia/Getty Images; p. 26 Jochen Sand/Photodisc/Thinkstock; p. 27 James Woodson/Digital Vision/Thinkstock; p. 28 Jupiterimages/Creatas/Thinkstock; p. 29 © www.iStockphoto.com/Kelly Cline; p. 30 David Sacks/Lifesize/Thinkstock.

Library of Congress Cataloging-in-Publication Data

Gosman, Gillian.
 Earth-friendly shopping / by Gillian Gosman. — 1st ed.
     p. cm. — (How to be Earth friendly)
 Includes index.
 ISBN 978-1-4488-2591-2 (library binding) — ISBN 978-1-4488-2771-8 (pbk.) — ISBN 978-1-4488-2772-5 (6-pack)
 1. Shopping—Juvenile literature. 2. Sustainable living—Juvenile literature. I. Title.
 TX335.5.G67 2011
 640—dc22

                                                      2010036765

Manufactured in the United States of America

CPSIA Compliance Information: Batch #WW11PK: For Further Information contact Rosen Publishing, New York, New York at 1-800-237-9932

CONTENTS

What Is Earth-Friendly Shopping?

Shopping at a small market that sells organic and locally grown foods is an Earth-friendly shopping choice.

What we buy can say a lot about what we value. Some people take the time to find and buy Earth-friendly, or green, goods. These people believe that the things they buy can and should be made in ways that do not harm the **environment**. Earth-friendly goods are products that are sustainable. Something is sustainable if it does not use up natural **resources** or make harmful waste.

Earth-friendly goods and services used to be hard to find. Lately, though, there has been a lot of interest in green products. Companies are using Earth-friendly methods to make new products. They are making more goods that are made to last and be reused or to **biodegrade** safely, too. Shopping for Earth-friendly goods helps our planet!

Earth-friendly shopping is not just about buying fruits and vegetables. It is important to pick appliances, such as refrigerators, that use energy well, too.

Why Buy Green?

People throw away tons of trash every day. This trash often ends up in a landfill like the one shown here.

We live in a world that likes things fast, cheap, and **disposable**. Think of how many paper cups, plastic bags, and glass jars you have thrown away after just one use. What about the other everyday things that fill our landfills, such as plastic pens, batteries, and packages for toys, food, electronics, cleaners, beauty products, and so on? These goods may make our lives easier in the short term. In the end, though, they could cost us money, our health, and the health of the planet.

Factories make more than 30 billion bottles of water each year. The amount of oil needed to produce these bottles could fuel one million cars for a year!

7

Think about a plastic bottle of water. It is a sunny day at the park, and you get thirsty. You buy a bottle of water, drink it, and toss it in the nearest trash can. You are not alone in doing this. About 40 million plastic bottles of water are thrown away every day!

Let's take a closer look at that waste. To make the plastic that was used in the bottle, a **fossil fuel** called petroleum must be drilled from the ground. Drilling **pollutes** the air and nearby waterways. After the bottle is

Using a reusable water bottle saves you money and it helps Earth!

made and filled with water, it is shipped many miles (km) to your local grocery store, wasting even more fossil fuel! Even after the bottle has been emptied, the

Recycling plastic and metal products means those things do not end up in landfills. Instead they are used again to make things people need or want.

plastic lasts. A plastic bottle can take 1,000 years to break down in a landfill. In the meantime, it will add to the piles of trash that are building up in these places. Was it worth the convenience?

Earth-Friendly Production

Companies are under pressure from the government and from shoppers to make changes that help Earth. This has caused many companies to create green **initiatives** to make their factories and offices Earth friendlier. These factories use less **nonrenewable** energy, create less waste, and recycle more of the

Some carmakers, such as Ford, try to balance out the harm they cause the environment by doing things to help Earth. The Ford headquarters is shown here.

waste they produce. Many green factories also return land once used to make products to its natural state. They also build machines that run on less power and provide a healthier environment for workers by having plenty of natural light and windows with views.

Just about any factory and any business can go green. The car companies Honda, Ford, and Volkswagen have North American factories that follow these initiatives. The New

Honda's Formula One racing team tried to fight global warming through its Earth Dreams program. The program raised money from fans and gave it to Earth-friendly causes.

Jersey factory where M&M candies are made has the largest **solar panel** system of any factory in the country. The solar panels at the M&M factory create about 20 percent of the energy the factory needs to run.

Kettle Foods potato chips are made in a factory partly powered by wind **turbines**. The factory's used cooking oil is also recycled into a fuel called **biodiesel**.

Steinway and Sons, the makers of world-famous pianos, also get a hand from the Sun. The company built a solar-powered heating and cooling system for their New York City factory. The Sun's heat is

This worker is putting solar panels on the roof of a large department store called Kohl's. The company has put panels on 100 stores as one of its many green initiatives.

caught by rows of curved mirrors on the factory's roof. The heat warms a pipe filled with water, turning it into steam, which can be used to heat the building.

Organic Foods and Cleaners

"Organic" is a word used to describe many products, from foods to fashions and carpets to cleaners. In general, it means goods and services that are made without harmful chemicals and with the

Only foods with the USDA seal, shown here, have been certified organic by the USDA.

least amount of waste. The United States Department of Agriculture (USDA) decides what foods can be advertised as organic. The USDA checks how the food was produced, how the crops were grown and harvested, how animals were treated, and how the food was carried from the farm or factory to the grocery store shelf.

The average piece of produce traveled 1,500 miles (2,414 km) to get to your local store! It takes a lot of energy to power and refrigerate a truck over that distance. For this reason, many Earth-friendly people are "locavores." This means they eat only food grown and then sold within 50 to 100 miles (80–161 km) of where they are.

Most of the food in grocery stores was brought there from across the country by trucks. These trucks use a great deal of gas and dirty the air.

Common cleaning supplies are made with dozens of harmful chemicals. These chemicals are believed to cause cancer, allergies, problems breathing, and changes in behavior. These ingredients are flushed down toilets, washed down sink drains, emptied into the trash, and sprayed in the air. They then make their way into the

This person is making his own cleaner with vinegar, water, and eucalyptus oil.

ground, into the waterways, and into Earth's atmosphere, where they hurt people, plants, and animals. Organic cleaning supplies are those made with natural, nontoxic ingredients, such as baking soda, cornstarch, lemon juice, mineral oil, and vinegar. Look for these ingredients or the Green Seal logo on the label. Green Seal is a nonprofit group that checks on the green claims of lots of household goods.

Earth-Friendly Machines

IT'S A FACT!

In 1992, the Environmental Protection Agency (EPA) created the Energy Star label to let customers know which products use the least energy. The Energy Star program continues today. Customers who bought Energy Star appliances saved a total of $17 billion on their energy bills in 2009!

This appliance has the Energy Star label on it. This sticker lets you know the appliance is energy efficient.

Do you have lights, clocks, televisions, radios, a computer, a toaster, a microwave, a refrigerator, a stove, a washer and dryer, and other appliances in your home? They all use energy provided by the power company. Depending on when and how these appliances were made and how you and your family use them, you may be wasting energy and money.

You can change that! Use compact fluorescent lightbulbs, which last 10 times longer than incandescent lightbulbs and use only 25 percent as much energy. Turn off lights as you leave a room. Do not hold the refrigerator door open either. Shut off your computer each night, too.

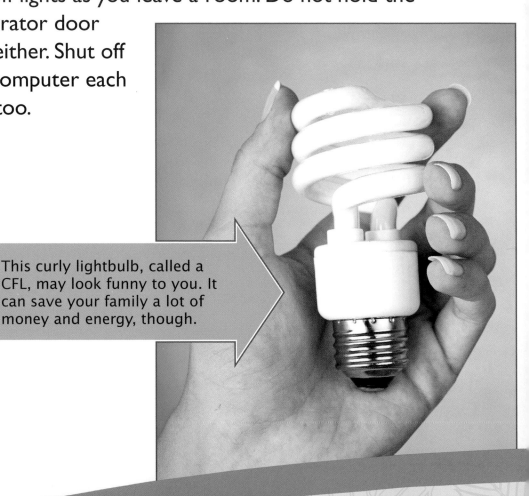

This curly lightbulb, called a CFL, may look funny to you. It can save your family a lot of money and energy, though.

The next time your family needs to replace an appliance, buy one that is Earth friendly! Every appliance must have an EnergyGuide label, which says how much energy it takes to run the appliance for a year and at what cost. Check and compare these labels.

When you hold open the refrigerator or freezer door, you let cold air out. Your refrigerator then has to work harder to cool things down again.

You Look Good in Green

You may see a picture like this one on cotton clothing labels. It tells you that the cotton is organic.

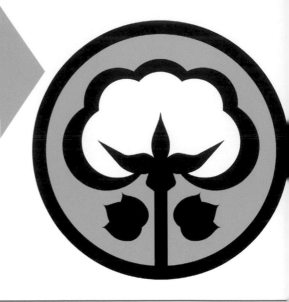

Did you know that even the clothes on your back may be hurting the environment? Cotton is one of the most popular **textiles.** You might wonder what could be wrong with a natural fiber. Most cotton is grown using pesticides, or chemicals used to kill pests. These chemicals make their way into the ground and the water, where they harm plants

Organic textiles can be just as beautiful as other textiles. Picking clothing made with organic cloth helps Earth, too!

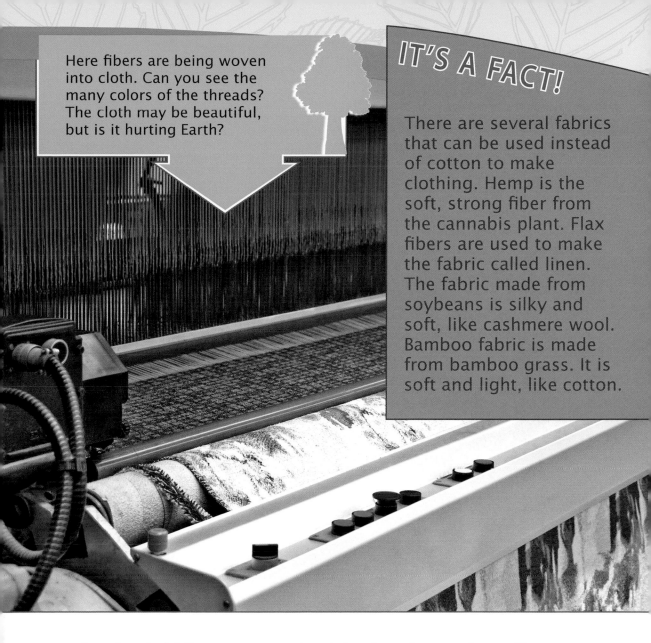

Here fibers are being woven into cloth. Can you see the many colors of the threads? The cloth may be beautiful, but is it hurting Earth?

IT'S A FACT!

There are several fabrics that can be used instead of cotton to make clothing. Hemp is the soft, strong fiber from the cannabis plant. Flax fibers are used to make the fabric called linen. The fabric made from soybeans is silky and soft, like cashmere wool. Bamboo fabric is made from bamboo grass. It is soft and light, like cotton.

and animals. When cotton is picked and spun into fibers, more chemicals are used to clean, bleach, and dye it. Just as many harmful chemicals go into making synthetic, or manmade, textiles, such as acrylic and spandex.

21

There are Earth-friendly clothes, though! Fibers made from organically grown plants, such as cotton, hemp, flax, bamboo, and soy, are used by all kinds of environmentally friendly clothing companies. Clothes are also made out of recycled materials. For example, Simple Shoes makes many of the soles for their shoes out of recycled car tires. Other companies make shoes from old pairs of jeans, purses from recycled plastic bags, and dresses from recycled neckties.

These rain boots are made from recycled PVC, which is a kind of plastic.

More Earth-Friendly Products

Clothes are not the only products made from recycled materials. Companies are creating new, Earth-friendly ways to make paper products, furniture, housewares, and building materials.

One popular construction material is recycled plastic made to look like wood. These "poly-woods" are used to make furniture, flooring, and other building supplies.

Some toy companies use sustainable woods and Earth-friendly paints to make their products.

Some stuffed animals have harmful chemicals in them. Many parents choose to buy toys that help Earth and are safe for their children.

Other companies are making tables and chairs from old newspapers and cardboard boxes. Reclaimed wood has also become very popular. Wood is collected from old barns, bowling alleys, and school gyms and used to build homes, furniture, and works of art.

These garden steps are made from recycled railroad ties.

Even toys are getting an Earth-friendly makeover. A toy company called Fuzz That Wuzz makes stuffed animals from recycled plastic bottles. The furry coat of each stuffed creature is made from 10 plastic bottles, which are cut into thin pieces and turned into polyester. The company Green Toys makes trucks, blocks, and other toys from recycled milk jugs.

25

Is It Really Earth Friendly?

It seems everyone is going green these days! Many companies want to cash in on the popularity of Earth-friendly products. They may not all be truly Earth friendly, though. In fact, some companies may be "greenwashing" their goods. Greenwashing is the practice of presenting

Read labels carefully to understand what you are buying. Some companies may say they are using organic things in their products, but are they using harmful chemicals, too?

IT'S A FACT!

If you are not sure what is in a product, visit the company's Web site and read closely. Most sustainable businesses are doing more than just using good ingredients in their products. What else are they doing to protect the environment and make products through sustainable practices?

It pays to be a smart shopper. One way to become one is to look up companies or brands on the Internet to find out what their business practices are.

a product as green even when it does little to help the environment and may even be very harmful.

Here is how you can tell whether a product is truly as Earth friendly as it seems. Look for the words "organic" and "recycled" on the label. If you see other green-sounding words on labels, such as "natural" and "nontoxic," be careful. These words are not regulated, or watched over, by the government or any other rule-making group. Any company can use these words to describe their product, even if they are not true. Look for the seal of one of the groups, such as the USDA, EnergyStar, or Green Seal, that regulates claims and labels. Finally, look at the list of ingredients. You need to be a smart shopper to be a good friend to Earth.

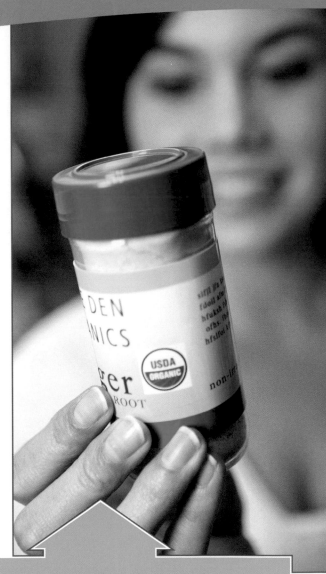

If you are not sure which food products are really green, choose ones with the USDA seal on them.

What can you do to show companies you really want to help our planet stay healthy? You can do plenty! Bring cloth bags to the grocery store instead of using

Reusable shopping bags, like this one, are a great way to help the environment. They can be used to carry many things besides groceries, too!

paper or plastic bags. Carry a reusable water bottle with you. Ask companies to stop sending you their printed advertisements in the mail, too. All those catalogs waste paper and energy.

Shop at local farmers' markets or farms. You will be supporting independent businesses. You will get fresh fruits and vegetables, too! Buy other goods from companies that are working hard for the environment.

That is just the beginning. If you put your mind to it, you can create the green products of the future!

Going to yard sales is an Earth-friendly alternative to buying things in a regular store. Yard sales can be lots of fun to explore, too.

GLOSSARY

biodegrade (by-oh-dih-GRAYD) To break down naturally over time.

biodiesel (by-oh-DEE-zel) A fuel that can power cars, trucks, buses, and other vehicles and is made from the oil from plants.

disposable (dih-SPOH-zuh-bel) Able to be thrown away.

environment (en-VY-ern-ment) Everything that surrounds human beings and other living things and everything that makes it possible for them to live.

fossil fuel (FO-sul FYOOL) A fuel, such as coal, natural gas, or gasoline, that is made from plants that died millions of years ago.

initiatives (ih-NIH-shuh-tivz) First steps in doing things.

nonrenewable (non-ree-NOO-uh-bul) Able to be used up.

pollutes (puh-LOOTS) Poisons with harmful matter.

resources (REE-sawrs-ez) Things that occur in nature and that can be used or sold, such as gold, coal, or wool.

solar panel (SOH-ler PA-nul) A collector that captures and stores solar energy.

textiles (TEK-stylz) Woven cloths.

turbines (TER-bynz) Motors that are turned by the flow of water, wind, or some other energy source.

INDEX

WEB SITES

Due to the changing nature of Internet links, PowerKids Press has developed an online list of Web sites related to the subject of this book. This site is updated regularly. Please use this link to access the list:
www.powerkidslinks.com/hbef/shop/